Eliminating Your Debt in 12 (x) Easy Steps and Keep Them Off

A Practical Guide To Eliminating Your Debt Forever!

[RS Johnson]

Copyright © 2012 **RS Johnson**

All rights reserved.

Table of Contents

Introduction 6

Chapter-01: Effective Strategies for Tackling Your Debt 7

    Stop Accumulating Debt 7

    Build an Emergency Fund 7

    Use the Debt Snowball Method 8

    Request a Lower Interest Rate from Your Creditor 8

    Increase Your Income 9

    Withdraw From Your Retirement Fund 9

    Cash Out a Life Insurance Policy 10

    Debt Settlement 10

    Credit Counseling 10

Chapter- 02: Steps to Be Debt-Free in Less Than a Year 12

    Bump up your debt repayment percentage 12

    Use savings to pay down larger debts 12

    Negotiate for a lower interest rate 12

    Pay off your debts with your tax refund. 13

    Sell items for cash 13

    Consider cashing in your life insurance 13

Make more money 14

Do a credit card balance transfer 14

To get rid of old debt, use a statute of limitations law. 14

To get your credit card debts discharged, file for bankruptcy. 15

Chapter-03: How to Pay Off Debt? 16

Strategies That Work 16

How Debt Affects Your Credit Scores 16

Why Is Credit Card Debt So Risky? 17

Chapter-04: Ways to Pay Off Debt on Multiple Cards 19

How Do I Use the Avalanche Method to Pay Off Debt? 20

Pros and Cons of the Debt Avalanche..............21

How Do I Use the Snowball Method to Pay Off Debt? 22

Example of the Debt Snowball in Action 23

Pros and Cons of the Debt Snowball 23

Chapter-05: How Personal Loans Impact Credit Scores 25

How Do Balance Transfers Help Me Pay Off Debt? 25

How Do I Use a Personal Loan to Pay Off Credit Card Debt? 26

Max Loan 28

How Do I Use Debt Settlement to Pay Off My Debt? 29

How Do I Get Out of Debt After Filing for Bankruptcy? 31

Conclusion 33

Introduction

With a mortgage, vehicle loan, school loans, credit cards, and medical costs, debt may quickly spiral out of control. Whether your debt results from a job loss, unforeseen costs, or overspending, you can lessen and finally eliminate it. Debt relief requires time and work, but you may effectively dig your way out of debt by combining techniques and remaining persistent. Here are some pointers to properly assist you in getting out of debt. While some of these measures may appear minor, such as avoiding additional debt and saving for an emergency, they are critical for establishing a solid financial foundation that will allow you to pay off your debt effectively. Tracking your progress along the way keeps you motivated and reminds you that you're getting closer to your debt-reduction objective.

Chapter-01: Effective Strategies for Tackling Your Debt

Stop Accumulating Debt

This method will not get you out of debt, but it will keep you from making it more difficult to repay. Reduce your incentive to incur further debt by discontinuing the use of your credit cards or even freezing your credit. Freezing your credit closes your credit reports to new queries, making it more difficult to apply for new credit on the spur of the moment. This procedure is generally meant to reduce identity theft, but it can also assist you in avoiding the establishment of new lines of credit.

If you do not have one already, now is the time to get one. A budget can properly help you align your spending with your income, allowing us to make the most of the dollar that comes in and keep you from relying on credit cards or loans to make ends meet.

Build an Emergency Fund

Putting money in an emergency fund may seem contradictory if you're trying to get out of debt—you might use that money to pay off your debt instead of putting it in a savings account—but an emergency fund can protect you from incurring further debt. In addition, these savings offer you a safety net that you may utilize for unexpected costs, preventing you from going for your credit card. The ideal emergency fund has six to twelve months' worth of living costs, but you may start with $1,000 or whatever you can manage to save.

Use the Debt Snowball Method

The less you pay each month toward your loan amounts, the longer it will take to pay them off. This is because interest may significantly lengthen the time it takes to repay your loan, and most debit accounts accrue interest charges every month. Many individuals believe that the debt snowball approach is an effective strategy to pay off debt. This strategy allows you to make significant progress by paying as much as possible toward your smallest amount each month. Meanwhile, make the minimum payment on your other debts to keep your accounts in good standing. Once you've paid off your lowest debt, go on to the next smallest sum, and so on until you have paid off all of your accounts. The debt avalanche approach is a debt-reduction strategy that differs from the debt-snowball method. Using this method, you would begin by making as many payments as possible toward the loan with the greatest interest rate. Then, after you paid it off, you would go to the debt with the next-highest interest rate, and so on.

Request a Lower Interest Rate from Your Creditor

Higher interest rates keep you in debt for a longer period since so much of your payment goes toward the monthly interest charge rather than the actual balance. On the other hand, interest rates are negotiable, and you may ask your credit card issuers to decrease your interest rate. Creditors do this at their discretion, so clients with solid payment histories have a better chance of negotiating reduced rates. By looking for specials, you may obtain a cheaper interest rate if you utilize a balance transfer to receive a cheaper interest rate and attempt to pay it off before the promotional rate ends. When the promotional period expires, your balance will be subject to higher interest rates. To qualify for a low-interest or debt transfer credit card, you generally need to have decent to outstanding credit.

Increase Your Income

The more cash you properly put toward your debt, the sooner you will be able to pay it off permanently. Look for methods to get more money to pay off your debts. You may, for example, make additional money by selling goods from your house, beginning a side business, or earning money from a pastime. If you negotiate a raise or work more hours at your full-time job, you may be able to earn more money.

Withdraw From Your Retirement Fund

In severe instances, you could consider withdrawing funds from your retirement account to pay off your debt. However, if you are under 59½, you will be subject to early withdrawal penalties and extra tax liabilities. The precise penalty you'll pay is determined by the retirement account you withdraw and how you spend the money, but the usual early withdrawal penalty is a 10% tax.

Furthermore, when it comes time to retire, your savings will be depleted—not only from the money you took out but also from the interest, dividends, and capital gains you could have made with that money. Borrowing from work-sponsored retirement plans, such as a 401(k), is an option (k). This technique, however, is fraught with danger. If you lose your work, you may be required to repay the loan in a shorter period, which may exacerbate your financial difficulties.

Cash Out a Life Insurance Policy

You could have some cash in your whole or universal life insurance policy that you can use to pay off your debt. However, this is a hazardous approach that may result in tax repercussions, similar to accessing retirement savings. In addition, cashing out implies that you are relinquishing your life insurance policy and is no longer in force. Borrowing from your insurance policy is another option, but it may impact the death payment your beneficiaries get.

Debt Settlement

Debt settlement may be an option if your accounts are overdue or you owe more money than you can properly repay over a few years. When you pay your debts, you ask the creditor for a one-time, lump-sum payment that is less than the total amount owed to clear the bill completely. Creditors generally accept settlement proposals only on accounts that are in default or on the verge of default. On the other hand, debt settlement can hurt your credit score and should only be utilized as a last resort. You may settle your bills on your own by negotiating directly with your creditors, or you can hire a professional debt relief firm to assist you. However, be wary of any firm that encourages you to intentionally fall behind on payments in the hopes of settling your debt once your accounts have gone into default.

Credit Counseling

Credit counseling companies are often non-profit organizations that can assist you in managing your money and debt. Certified credit counselors work with creditors on your behalf to establish an inexpensive debt management plan when it comes to debt repayment. You will submit a lump sum payment to the credit counseling organization each month, which will split the money and distribute it to your creditors on your behalf. A debt management plan developed with a credit counselor is not the same as debt settlement in that you do not have to be in default for credit counseling, and the aim is to pay your debts in full. The National Foundation for Credit Counseling can properly help you identify a credit counselor. Both organizations provide credit counseling services through local member agencies.

Chapter- 02: Steps to Be Debt-Free in Less Than a Year

Bump up your debt repayment percentage

Putting at least 15% of your paycheck — or income from Social Security or pensions — toward credit card debt and loans can help you pay them off considerably faster because most credit card issuers only need you to pay around 2% of the outstanding sum each month. Making tiny, minimal payments implies that your loan amounts are accruing interest month after month or year after year. Paying off huge portions of debt in a few months might save you a lot of money only on interest payments.

Use savings to pay down larger debts

Don't be hesitant to spend some of your money to pay down high-interest loans. Using cash reserves to settle debt is a wise option because you will no longer be incurring interest on those big sums. Although having some extra cash in your bank account may seem reassuring, the fact is that that money isn't working for you - not with today's record-low interest rates. Don't exhaust all of your savings.

Negotiate for a lower interest rate

Call your creditors and ask for a reduced interest rate. You'd be amazed at how many creditors are prepared to lower your interest rate based on your payment history and account status.

If you have a long-term relationship with someone, you may be in a much better position to qualify for a lower interest rate. This can properly save you money on interest payments as you pay off your debt over the year.

Pay off your debts with your tax refund.

While it may be tempting to splurge on a high-priced item or go on vacation with your tax refund, a wiser financial move would be to pay off part, or all, of your debt. Consider the benefit of lowering your monthly payments with a single lump sum debt repayment approach. Instead of enjoying the short-term delight of purchase, you'll reap the benefits of a reduced debt load over the year and for years to come.

Sell items for cash

Make a list of goods that you might be able to sell on eBay, Craigslist, or at a garage sale. Drumming up some extra cash by selling goods you no longer need or are willing to part with — and then utilizing the proceeds to pay off debt — can help you quickly reduce your debt burden.

Consider cashing in your life insurance

Cashing in your life insurance policy may be a wise debt-reduction strategy because it allows you to pay off larger sums of debt more quickly. If you are properly drowning in debt and have no beneficiaries, who need to benefit from your life insurance payouts, such as a husband or children, using the cash to pay off debt may make sense.

If you have a proper term life insurance policy, this method does not apply to you. It only applies to people who have whole life insurance with a cash value. However, even if you have beneficiaries, you may be able to access some of the cash value of your whole life policy, allowing you to pay off debt while still leaving some life insurance profits to your loved ones.

Make more money

If you are properly committed to paying off your debt within a year, you should search for methods to boost your income and utilize that extra money to pay off your debt as soon as possible. For example, consider taking up a part-time job or negotiating a raise with your company to generate extra money for at least a few months while making debt reduction a top priority.

Do a credit card balance transfer

Most of us shred all credit card debt transfers that appear in our mailboxes. However, if you want to accelerate your debt-reduction efforts, a balance transfer might assist. Transferring high-interest debt to a zero-interest agreement — one that lasts for a year or so – eliminates all credit-card charges. This frees up cash flow, allowing you more money to pay off your credit card debts. Just make sure to read the tiny print before joining up to ensure you're getting the cheap rate.

To get rid of old debt, use a statute of limitations law.

Some people pay off old credit card bills, even though they are no longer legally required to do so. We're all eager to pay our debts. However, suppose money is particularly tight, and you don't have it. In that case, you should prioritize current payments and consider preceding repayment of old invoices that are 8 to 10 years old or even longer.

Each state has its own set of regulations when it comes to outstanding debts. For example, some jurisdictions prohibit debt collectors from collecting a certain sort of debt after a particular length of time. In contrast, others limit the amount of time a creditor may sue you over an old debt. In any case, you should check to see if the statute of limitations on an old obligation you may owe has expired. If it has passed, you can probably avoid payments without fear of financial, legal, or credit penalties.

For additional information on dealing with old debts, contact your state Attorney General or a consumer protection agency for assistance and guidance on your state's credit card debt statute of limitations.

To get your credit card debts discharged, file for bankruptcy.

However, in severe cases, such as when you have no income or have unmanageable credit card payments or medical expenditures, a Chapter 7 bankruptcy petition is suitable to discharge all credit card obligations. In addition, if you feel ethically compelled to repay your debts, you may want to consider Chapter 13, which decreases part of your credit card costs. The remainder of the loan is then repaid over a three- to five-year period.

Chapter-03: How to Pay Off Debt?

Strategies That Work

Debt may be daunting, especially if you owe money on several credit cards. But, with these techniques, you can regain control, know you're making progress toward debt repayment, and save money on interest.

Debt may be a four-letter word in more ways than one.

When it spirals out of control, whether due to medical expenses, shopping sprees, or unforeseen crises, it becomes an albatross that threatens your emotional and physical health; although it may appear daunting, you can approach every debt in the same manner: one step at a time. So here's a guide to paying off debt — specifically, credit card debt — even when it seems impossible.

Begin by studying what debt may do to your credit score and why credit card debt is especially detrimental. Or try our favorite debt-reduction strategy, the debt avalanche.

How Debt Affects Your Credit Scores

The first thing you properly need to think about is that debt has ramifications throughout your entire financial life, including your credit ratings.

This article will go over two forms of debt: revolving and installment. Credit cards are the most common source of revolving debt because you may carry, or revolve, a balance from month to month. You may borrow as much money as you want, up to a specified credit limit, and interest rates are variable. Therefore, your monthly payment on revolving debt may vary based on how much you presently owe.

Mortgages, vehicle loans, school loans, and personal loans all contribute to installment debt. In most situations, the amount borrowed, the interest rate and the size of your monthly payments are all determined at the outset.

Both types of debt must be paid off on time. When you miss a payment, your lender may report it to credit bureaus, and this information can stay on your credit report for up to seven years. You may also be required to pay late fees, which will have no effect on your credit score but can be inconvenient.

Aside from your payment history, each type of debt has a distinct impact on your credit. A substantial amount of installment debt, such as student loans and mortgages, has little impact on your credit. Revolving debt, on the other hand, is an entirely different matter. Suppose you maintain large amounts on your credit cards relative to your credit limits from month to month. In that case, it will most certainly hurt your credit ratings – especially if you do it with numerous cards. Because the amount of available credit you utilize — also known as credit usage — is heavily weighted in determining your credit scores, it can harm your credit. To keep your credit score high, keep your credit card amounts as low as possible. Ideally, you should pay off the whole balance of your statements each month.

Why Is Credit Card Debt So Risky?

When it properly comes to debt, credit card debt is frequently the most sinister.

Credit card companies may entice you with a low introductory APR and a sparkling credit line. However, the promotional APR deal will expire at some point. If you don't handle your new credit card account properly, you may find yourself staring at an enormous mountain of debt when it happens.

Because credit card interest rates are generally quite high, revolving debt may be extremely daunting. So, if you make the minimum payment each month, it will take you a long time — potentially decades — to pay off your amount. You'll also be paying a lot of interest throughout that period. Assume you charge $8,000 on a credit card with a 17 percent APR and then put the card in a drawer, never spending another dime. If you simply pay the minimum amount on that account each month, it might take you almost 16 years to pay it off – and cost you nearly $7,000 in interest (depending on the terms of your agreement).

Chapter-04: Ways to Pay Off Debt on Multiple Cards

Are you ready to pay off your debt? The first step is to devise a debt repayment strategy.

If you simply have one loan, your plan should be straightforward: make the largest monthly debt payment you can afford. Then, rinse and repeat until everything is gone. However, if you are like most individuals in debt, you have several accounts to handle. In such a case, you'll need to identify the debt-reduction strategy that works best for you.

Many people use the debt snowball and debt avalanche techniques advocated by financial expert Dave Ramsey. Both of these techniques and alternatives like balance transfers, personal loans, and bankruptcy will be discussed more below. When you want to decrease the amount of interest you pay on numerous credit cards, we propose adopting the debt avalanche approach. If that method isn't for you, there are numerous options to explore.

1. Snowball Method
2. Avalanche Method
3. Balance Transfers
4. Debt Settlement
5. Personal Loans
6. Bankruptcy

How Do I Use the Avalanche Method to Pay Off Debt?

With this debt-reduction technique, also known as debt stacking, you will pay off your accounts in the sequence of greatest interest rate to the lowest interest rate. This is how it works:

- Pay the bare minimum on all of your accounts.
- Put as much money as you can into the account with the greatest interest rate.
- Once you've paid off the loan with the highest interest rate, start paying as much as you can on the next highest interest rate account. Then, continue the process until all of your debts have been paid off.

When you pay off one account, you free up more money each month to apply to the next obligation. You'll also pay less overall and get out of debt faster if you tackle your obligations in order of interest rate. It may take some time to see anything happen, similar to an avalanche. However, once you acquire traction, your debts will fall away like a rushing wall of snow.

Example of the Debt Avalanche in Action

Assume you have four distinct types of debts:
Type of Debt Balance Interest Rate (APR)
Auto Loan $15,000 4.5%
Student Loan $25,000 5.5%
Credit Card $7,000 22.0%
Personal Loan $5,000 10.0%
To employ the debt avalanche approach, follow these steps:
1. Order the debts from greatest to the lowest interest rate.

2. Always make the monthly minimum payment on each account.
3. Put any excess money toward the account with the highest interest rate, which is the credit card.
4. Once you have properly paid off your credit card debt, utilize the money you were paying towards paying down the next highest interest rate - the personal loan.
5. Once you've paid off the personal loan, add the amount you've been paying to your student loan installments.
6. Once the school loan is paid off, add the money you've been putting toward other obligations to your vehicle loan installments.

As a result, you'll wind up paying off your accounts in the following order:
1. Credit Card ($7,000)
2. Student Loan ($25,000)
3. Auto Loan ($15,000)
4. Personal loan ($5,000)

Pros and Cons of the Debt Avalanche

The debt avalanche will assist you in paying less interest and getting out of debt more quickly. You'll also get a rush from seeing the highest interest rates vanish first.

As a result, we prefer the debt avalanche method of debt repayment.

What's the snag? It will properly take more time to see results than the debt snowball. So, if you rely on small victories to keep you motivated, the following technique might be a better fit for you.

How Do I Use the Snowball Method to Pay Off Debt?

You'll use the debt snowball to pay off your obligations in the order of the smallest balance to the highest. This is how it works:

- Pay the bare minimum on all of your accounts.
- Put as much more money as you can into the account with the lowest balance.
- When your smallest debt is paid off, redirect the money you put toward it to your next lowest loan. Then, continue the process until all of your debts have been paid off.

Many individuals like this strategy because it involves a succession of modest victories at the start, which will motivate you to pay off the balance of your debt. The debt snowball approach also can enhance your credit scores more rapidly by lowering your credit usage on individual credit cards sooner and reducing the number of accounts with outstanding amounts.

Using this method, you prioritize your smallest amount first, regardless of interest rates. Then, when that is paid off, you go to the account with the next lowest balance.

Consider a snowball rolling over the ground: It may gather up more and more snow as it grows in size. Each amount cleared offers you extra money to help you pay off the following one faster. When you pay off your smaller bills initially, those paid-off accounts provide you with the desire to continue paying off debt.

Furthermore, the debt snowball approach may have an immediate favorable influence on your credit ratings (especially if you eliminate credit card debt first). Better credit can also help you save money in other aspects of your life.

Example of the Debt Snowball in Action

Let's utilize the same accounts as in the previous example.
Type of Debt Balance Interest Rate (APR)
Credit Card $7,000 22.0%
Auto Loan $15,000 4.5%
Personal Loan $5,000 10.0%
Student Loan $25,000 5.5%

To employ the debt snowball approach, follow these steps:
1. Order the debts from lowest to greatest balance.
2. Always make the monthly minimum payment on each account.
3. Apply any additional funds to the loan with the lowest balance — the personal loan.
4. Once you've paid off the personal loan, utilize the money you put towards it to pay down the next smallest sum - the credit card debt.
5. Once the credit card is paid off, add the money you've been paying to your vehicle loan installments.
6. Once the vehicle loan is paid off, add the money you've been paying to your student loan installments.

Using the debt snowball approach, you will pay off your accounts in the following order:
1. Personal loan ($5,000)
2. Auto Loan ($15,000)
3. Credit Card ($7,000)
4. Student Loan ($25,000)

Pros and Cons of the Debt Snowball

If you have many local debts to pay off or need the motivation to pay a huge amount of debt, the debt snowball may be a good fit. For example, assume you have multiple credit card balances and cannot qualify for a new balance transfer card to consolidate your revolving debt properly. In that case, this could be an option.

When you are dealing with a mountain of debt, this method allows you to see results as soon as possible. You may clear your mind of that account by removing the lowest, simplest balance first. Reducing the number of accounts on your credit reports with outstanding amounts may also boost your credit ratings.

The main disadvantage of the snowball approach is that it usually costs more in the long run than the avalanche method. Because you do not account for interest rates, you may find yourself paying off higher-interest accounts later. That extra time will cost you more money in interest. While the debt snowball and onslaught are two general debt-reduction strategies, here are some specific approaches you can use in conjunction with them.

Chapter-05: How Personal Loans Impact Credit Scores

How Do Balance Transfers Help Me Pay Off Debt?

Once you have credit card debt, you can transfer the balance to another card.

If you have a high-interest account, you can transfer the funds to a card with a lower interest rate and pay less money in interest over time. This is equivalent to repaying one credit card with another.

- Determine which credit cards you are paying interest on.
- Determine how much money you can or want to send.
- Apply for a new cashback credit card with a 0% APR on debt transfers for a set period (or find a balance transfer offer on a card you already have).
- Transfer the balance (or amounts) from the previous cards to the new card.
- Pay off your new card's balance as soon as possible; attempt to do so before the 0% interest term expires.

After completing a balance transfer, you will increase the credit limits on those cards; but, do not utilize your newly available credit to incur further debt.

A lower-interest balance transfer card can complement the avalanche approach. Because a balance transfer may be used to lower the interest rate on your highest-interest loan deliberately, it can allow you time to work on the next-highest-interest account. This can lower the overall amount of interest you pay.

Many debt transfer credit cards even offer 0% APR for a limited time (typically 6–18 months). A 0% APR deal allows you to pay off your credit card amount without incurring additional interest charges.

Assume you have $6,000 in credit card debt with an 18% APR. You might move the debt to a card with a 0% APR for 12 months. You would save more than $600 in interest if you paid off your loan within that period.

According to the 2020 Credit Card Insider study results, 78 percent of U.S. consumers who have done balance transfers feel that they were beneficial. Balance transfers are a great solution if you can keep to a strict payment schedule. However, they are not for everyone. However, a few credit cards offer 0% APR debt transfers with no balance transfer fees. If you have strong credit, you may be able to get a favorable balance transfer deal. Check out our recommendations for the best balance transfer cards to save money.

How Do I Use a Personal Loan to Pay Off Credit Card Debt?

Generally, paying off credit card debt in full is the best financial approach. However, if you have so much credit card debt that you can't afford to send a huge check, and the debt avalanche technique appears too daunting or sluggish to manage, it may be time to seek another route.

Paying off several cards (and statements and due dates) using a low-interest personal loan might be a smart option in instances when you have numerous different cards.

- Do some research on different loan providers (see the tool below) to determine what rates you're likely to obtain and what fees you'll have to pay. A

consolidation loan may be a great choice if you can acquire a lower rate than you are now paying and pay less in fees.
- Apply for a personal loan from your preferred lender. You may be required to give credit card details so that the loan provider can directly pay your card issuers. They will send the funds to your bank account in certain circumstances, and you will be responsible for paying off your credit cards yourself.
- Repay the personal loan in accordance with its terms. You will be able to get out of debt faster and save money if you can pay more than the standard rate amount each month.

The following are some of the advantages of taking this route:
- **Consolidating consumer debt with a personal loan could help your credit score:** Because a private loan is an installment loan, the balance-to-limit ratio does not affect your credit in the same way that revolving accounts (such as credit cards) do. So, if you don't currently have any installment loans on your credit reports, paying off your credit card debt with an installment loan might dramatically improve your credit.
- **Overload can be alleviated with a personal loan:** When you use a personal loan to reduce the number of fees you have to make each month, debt management may become much easier.
- **Paying down credit card debt with a low-interest personal loan can save you money in the following ways:** The interest rate on a personal loan is frequently cheaper than the interest rate on a credit card. Therefore, if you qualify for a lower interest

installment loan, you will wind up paying less money in total.

Keep the loan terms in mind at all times, or you may end up making matters worse. If you don't trust yourself to utilize credit properly, stay away from this method. Otherwise, you risk being even more in debt.

If you adopt this technique, keep the following considerations in mind:

1. **Keep credit cards open:** If the credit cards you pay off have annual fees you don't wish to pay, don't shut them. Keep them open to help you make better use of your credit.
2. **Cut back on credit card spending:** Spend no more money on your prepaid credit cards. If necessary, conceal them or chop them up.
3. **Be a responsible borrower:** Make on-time payments on your installment loan. If you don't, you'll only make things worse for your credit.

Max Loan

Please keep in mind that we have not reviewed all of the providers included in this comparison tool because they are continuously changing. We may properly earn an affiliate commission if you obtain a loan via one of these services.

Here is a non-exhaustive list of alternative online lenders to consider (and we may receive a commission if you obtain a loan via one of these links):

- Upgrade Personal Loans
- SoFi Personal Loans

More comprehensive services, such as Debt.com, will improve the process and properly help you determine whether debt consolidation, bankruptcy, or other options are the best fit for you. Still, these will almost certainly come with additional fees for things you could do yourself.

How Do I Use Debt Settlement to Pay Off My Debt?

When you are properly ready to get rid of your credit card debt, another alternative to explore is debt settlement. This method is generally effective for those who (a) are already behind on their credit card payments and (b) can afford to make significant, one-time settlement payments to their creditors.

You may settle your debts independently or engage a professional debt settlement business to do it for you. If you properly decide to use a third party, do your homework to prevent fraudsters and excessive prices. Hiring a business to accomplish this is not essential and may wind up costing you far more money. Visit the FTC Consumer Information page to learn what to look out for.

- Examine your debts to see if you'll be able to repay them over time.
- Suppose you believe your obligations are overwhelming and have determined that bankruptcy is not the best option. In that case, you can try debt settlement on your own or contact a debt settlement business. The worse your position (more late payments or delinquencies), the more leverage you may have since your creditors will recognize that you are less likely to pay them in full.

If you go the DIY route:
- Contact each creditor and inform them that you are willing to settle your debt for a lower amount than the present sum. Maintain a low initial offer. It might be beneficial to save some money ahead of time to be in a better negotiation position.
- Be prepared for some wrangling with your creditors. The procedure might be time-consuming
- When you reach a settlement arrangement that you can live with, get it in writing. Don't provide any bank account or payment details until the agreement is signed.
- Pay down your settled debt, preferably for a considerably lower amount than the initial total.

Alternatively, if you want to engage with a debt settlement firm:
- Make a selection of debt settlement firms after researching them.
- Inquire with each firm about their general procedure, the estimated schedule, and how much they charge (you may find vast price differences).
- When you locate the ideal business for you and sign an agreement, they will tell you what to do next. Although the settlement business will generally manage all interactions with your creditors, you will most likely have to deal with curious phone calls and letters from those creditors for some time.
- The debt settlement business may request that you cease paying your creditors and instead put payments into an escrow account. After your creditors agree to settle for less than the sum, the escrow account will be utilized to pay them off.

- When a suitable offer comes in, the debt settlement business will utilize the cash in the escrow account to pay off your creditor, preferably for considerably less than the initial sum.

Debt settlement is a discussion in which a creditor, such as a credit card company or collections agency, agrees to take a partial payment rather than the entire sum to repay your credit card debt. You may be eligible if you have faced adversity such as job loss, physical issues, or divorce. Some creditors, however, will accept debt settlement even if you do not have any particular mitigating circumstances. This option is typically only accessible if it's apparent that you've been struggling to pay your expenses, such as if you've begun to accrue late payments or haven't been paying at all. When you settle your debt, you may be able to pay half or less of the initial sum.

How Do I Get Out of Debt After Filing for Bankruptcy?

When you've reached your breaking point and have nowhere else to turn, filing for bankruptcy might provide a fresh start. However, you should only use it as a last choice because bankruptcy may ruin your credit. Bankruptcy cannot be summarized in a few simple steps. However, the basic procedure is as follows:
- Examine your debts to see if you'll be able to repay them over time.
- If you believe your obligations are overwhelming and have determined that bankruptcy is the best option for you, look for bankruptcy attorneys in your region.
- When you locate the proper attorney, they will advise you on what you should do. You must provide

detailed evidence of your debts, credit cards, loans, bank accounts, and other financial products, as well as information on your assets and personal property. And there's more!
- The attorney will collect your information, and the bankruptcy will be filed with the appropriate authorities.
- When the bankruptcy is discharged, the creditors will write off the included debts, and you will no longer be liable for them. Depending on the kind of bankruptcy, it might be dismissed after 3–4 months or 3–5 years of filing.

Personal bankruptcy is classified into two types:
1. This frequently necessitates the surrender of some of your possessions.
2. As a result, you can keep your property.

Declaring any form of bankruptcy may be a lengthy and costly procedure, including attorney and court filing fees, and should not be undertaken carelessly. You must also obtain credit counseling that the Department has approved of Justice before filing for bankruptcy. Although you may handle the procedure on your own, it is preferable to hire an attorney.

Conclusion

Consider a large project you've meant to do. It may be a house remodeling, garage organization, or a job or school task. On the other hand, some jobs appear so onerous that it is simpler to put them off for as long as possible. Many people are struggling to pay off their debts because they also deal with them in this manner. They put off reading the mail, answering the phone, or making a plan for so long that when they finally sit down and assess their situation, they have no idea where to begin. As tempting as it is to properly believe that the garage will sort itself, one of the most effective ways to tackle a large project is to divide it into smaller, manageable pieces. This is also true when it comes to debt relief.

Consider what it properly takes to grow a crop of fruits or vegetables if you need more proof that all of your small changes add up. The gardener does not plant the seeds one day and then returns the following day to harvest the crop. The plants require time to mature. The gardener should take care of the soil by fertilizing it, directing or trimming the plants as they grow, and watering it. Gardeners must also rely on factors that are beyond their control, such as sunlight and rain. Some seasons are better than others, but in the end, a dedicated gardener's minute, meticulous activities pay off with a healthy harvest. Budgeting is a lot like gardening. Small changes take time to pile up. Debt repayment takes time. And, on occasion, we are confronted with situations over which we have no control. However, in the end, we reap what we sow.

<-*END*->

www.ingramcontent.com/pod-product-compliance
Lightning Source LLC
Chambersburg PA
CBHW070845220526
45466CB00002B/890